"Calm Canvas:Blissful Coloring Escapes"

€ 2024 by Selena L.L. Arnold All rights reserved.

Unauthorized use or reproduction of any portion of this book is strictly prohibited without the author's prior written consent, except for brief quotations allowed for book reviews.

ISBN/SKU: 979-8-8691-5219-0

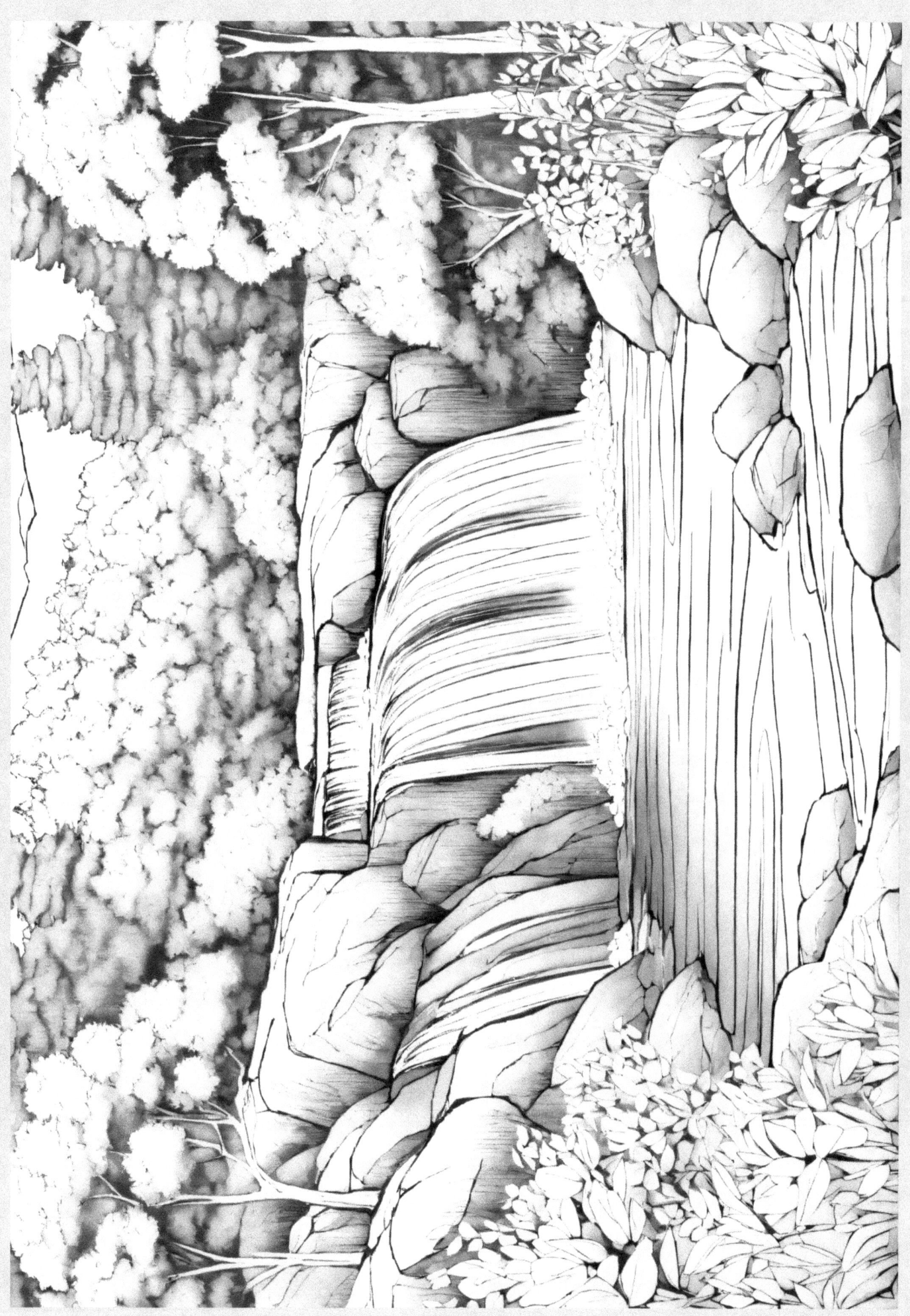